Original title:
In the Quiet

Copyright © 2024 Swan Charm
All rights reserved.

Author: Liisi Lendorav
ISBN HARDBACK: 978-9916-89-982-3
ISBN PAPERBACK: 978-9916-89-983-0
ISBN EBOOK: 978-9916-89-984-7

And Then, There Was Silence

The wind whispered low, in a soft, gentle sigh,
As shadows elongated, fading away into the night.
Stars blinked above, like secrets held tight,
And the world held its breath, in the calm of twilight.

Leaves rustled softly, beneath the pale moon,
A lullaby echoed, a sweet, haunting tune.
Time slowed its march, each moment a gift,
In the stillness, hearts stirred, began to lift.

The quiet embraced all, a tender caress,
Echoes of laughter, now distant, but blessed.
Memories lingered, like dust in the rays,
Of a twilight that promised, endless yesterdays.

Reflections danced gently on waters so clear,
In the peace of the night, lost whispers appeared.
Silent confessions, without the need for words,
In the tranquil embrace, the soul of the birds.

And then, there was silence, a moment divine,
In the heart of the void, where dreams intertwine.
With no sound to shatter, the stars shining bright,
In the garden of stillness, we found pure light.

Quietude's Gentle Touch

In the stillness of the night,
A whisper trails through the air.
The world wrapped in soft embrace,
Tranquility, beyond compare.

Stars murmur secrets untold,
Moonlight dances on the stream.
Every shadow, every fold,
Holds a softly spoken dream.

Gentle breeze sways the trees,
Nature's voice sings sweetly low.
Leaves flutter with quiet ease,
The heart learns to ebb and flow.

Time slows down, a soft retreat,
Moments linger like a sigh.
In this space, the world feels sweet,
Underneath the endless sky.

Quietude, a tender hand,
Cradles thoughts in soothing grace.
In this peace, we understand,
Love resides in this soft place.

Emptiness of the Mind

In the void where thoughts take flight,
Silence stretches, vast and wide.
A canvas pure, free of blight,
The soul's depth, where fears subside.

Drifting in the endless space,
Echoes fade, no longer near.
In the stillness, we find grace,
Emptiness holds what we fear.

Clouds of worry float away,
The heart learns to breathe anew.
In this calm, we slowly sway,
Finding peace in quiet views.

Thoughts surrender to the night,
Stars awaken in the haze.
In this gentle, tender light,
Life unfolds in tranquil ways.

Emptiness, a sacred gift,
Space to grow, to breathe, to dream.
In its arms, our spirits lift,
Finding joy in the unseen stream.

A Symphony of Silence

In the hush of fading light,
A symphony begins to rise.
Gentle notes in soft twilight,
Play beneath the whispering skies.

Each moment holds a heartbeat,
Nature's pulse in every breath.
A melody, pure and sweet,
Dance of life that conquers death.

Crickets chirp a soothing song,
The night carries them afar.
In the silence, we belong,
Underneath a watchful star.

Rustling leaves, a tender tune,
Stars punctuate the darkened dome.
In this space, beneath the moon,
We find harmony as home.

Symphony of moments shared,
The quiet breath of shared repose.
In our hearts, we are ensnared,
In the silence, love only grows.

The Peace of Unseen Corners

In corners where shadows weave,
Quiet dreams begin to bloom.
Silence whispers, softly grieve,
In the stillness, find your room.

Forgotten spaces hold their sighs,
Where glimpses of calm reside.
In these places, time defies,
The clamor of the world outside.

Dust motes dance in filtered light,
Carpets worn by gentle tread.
Hushed reflections take their flight,
In corners where the heart is led.

Peace lays softly on the floor,
Cushioned by the weight of years.
In these unseen corners' lore,
We find solace through our tears.

Unspoken truths in every fold,
In every quiet, hidden plea.
The peace of stories yet untold,
Waits patiently for you and me.

Echoes of Forgotten Thoughts

In whispers low, shadows creep,
Lost dreams in corners, secrets weep.
Fleeting moments, caught in time,
Silent echoes of thoughts in rhyme.

A flicker of light, a shadow's dance,
Memories swirl in a trance.
Once vibrant life, now fading grey,
Echoes linger, teasing stray.

Time unravels like fragile thread,
Words we spoke, now left unsaid.
In the stillness, we reflect,
Forgotten thoughts we might collect.

Through the mist of what once was near,
Longing whispers, ever clear.
In the heart's depth, stories lie,
Echoes beckon, never die.

Solitary Harmonies

In solitude's embrace, I find,
A melody that calms the mind.
Each note a breath, a heartbeat true,
Whispers of self, both old and new.

Underneath the starry sky,
A symphony of sighs, I try.
The silence sings a gentle tune,
As night unfolds, inviting moon.

Harmony in shadows plays,
A dance of light through dusky rays.
Loneliness wraps like a warm shawl,
In quiet moments, I hear it all.

Each strum of hope, a soothing balm,
In solitary spaces, I feel the calm.
A heart at peace, a soul that's free,
In these harmonies, I just be.

The Language of Inaction

In stillness lies a quiet power,
Moments linger, soft as a flower.
Words unspoken, thoughts set free,
Inaction sings a melody.

A pause before the world can change,
Life's rhythm finds a space to range.
Silent breaths hold weight profound,
Amidst the noise, a softer sound.

Time elongates in thoughtful care,
With each heartbeat, burdens bare.
Inaction's grace, a hidden art,
An invitation to restart.

Finding peace in quietude,
A moment's solace, a gentler mood.
In life's tempest, we stand still,
The language of inaction, a sacred will.

Breaths Held in Reverence

In the sacred hush of dawn,
A breath of stillness, a spirit drawn.
Nature whispers a silent prayer,
In reverence, we find our care.

The earth awakens, soft and slow,
In every heartbeat, love will grow.
Holding breath as light appears,
We honor moments, calm our fears.

Each sigh a testament to grace,
We find our peace in this shared space.
With every pause, a world unfolds,
In held breaths, the heart beholds.

Through every inhale, wisdom flows,
In sacred stillness, connection grows.
Breaths held softly, hearts in sync,
In reverence, we pause and think.

The Sound of Silence

In the hush of night, whispers fade,
Echoes linger, softly shared,
Footsteps lost in the stillness,
Embraced by shadows, unprepared.

Rustling leaves tell tales untold,
Silhouettes dance in muted grace,
Voices drown in the surrounding cold,
Silence wraps us in its embrace.

A heartbeat slows, time stands still,
Moments stretch, breathe in the dark,
Each thought floats, a drifting chill,
In this quiet, we ignite a spark.

Stars above shimmer like dreams,
Fleeting wishes hang in the air,
Blending fears with silent screams,
In the dark, we find our prayer.

Lost in reverie, senses cease,
A world outside falls away,
In silence, we find our peace,
A sanctuary where we stay.

Gentle Shadows

Softly they glide, shadows play,
In the light of the fading day,
A fleeting moment, day to night,
They dance around, a whispered flight.

Under the trees, they weave and spin,
Caressing the earth, where dreams begin,
Closing their eyes, they blend with dusk,
In the cool air, there's magic and husk.

Gentle caress on weary skin,
The warmth of twilight pulls us in,
Underneath the stars, they twirl,
Swaying softly, they form and swirl.

In quiet corners, secrets lie,
Among the shadows, hopes can fly,
Touch of twilight, when all seems still,
Gentle whispers, the heart can fill.

As night descends, their beauty glows,
Embracing worlds no one else knows,
Through shadows deep, we'll find our way,
Guided by whispers till break of day.

A Moment of Tranquility

In stillness lies a fragile peace,
Where worries fade and sorrows cease,
The air is soft, the sun dips low,
In this moment, time moves slow.

Gentle breezes brush the face,
Nature's embrace, a warm embrace,
With every breath, we find our ground,
In quietude, life's joys abound.

Rippling waters sing a tune,
As shadows stretch beneath the moon,
In the calm where spirits soar,
We touch a realm we can't ignore.

Nature hums a soothing sound,
In tranquil moments, we are found,
Through whispered thoughts and laughing trees,
We savor life with perfect ease.

A fleeting glimpse of what is true,
A moment shared between me and you,
In tranquility, we learn to dwell,
In silent peace, all is well.

Reflections in the Calm

On still waters, dreams unfold,
Mirrored visions, tales retold,
Glimmering stars meet that quiet shore,
In tranquil depths, we seek much more.

Ripples dance with gentle grace,
Echoing whispers in time and space,
A silent world where thoughts align,
In calm reflections, we intertwine.

Amid the silence, spirits sing,
In peaceful moments, our hearts take wing,
With every glance, new worlds arise,
In the calm, we find the wise.

Look within, the beauty flows,
Each quiet heartbeat softly glows,
In solitude, we craft our fate,
In calm reflections, we resonate.

A tranquil breath, the night unfolds,
In mirrored peace, the heart consoled,
Through every wave, we find our way,
In stillness, we learn to stay.

Caress of the Gentle Breeze

Whispers dance through emerald leaves,
A soft embrace where nature weaves.
Sunlight plays on slumbering grass,
Time slows down as moments pass.

Cotton clouds drift lazily by,
An open heart beneath the sky.
With every breath, the world stands still,
A tranquil tune, a perfect thrill.

Birdsongs echo, sweet and clear,
Nature's voice, it's all we hear.
In this haven, worries cease,
A gentle touch, a sense of peace.

The winding path, a lover's trace,
Through blooming flowers, hearts embrace.
In every rustle, every sigh,
Life awakens, and so do I.

Underneath the old oak tree,
Dancing shadows set me free.
Breezes, tender, light as air,
In their arms, I lose my care.

Moments Wrapped in Silence

In the quiet, whispers bloom,
Softly weaving through the room.
Time stands still, a sacred space,
Filling hearts with gentle grace.

The tick of clocks feels far away,
Lost in thoughts, we gently sway.
In every pause, the world unfolds,
Hidden stories waiting, untold.

A tender glance, a knowing smile,
Moments linger, for a while.
Silence speaks in muted tones,
Resting softly in our bones.

Embraced by shadows of the night,
Stars above, a guiding light.
In this silence, dreams take flight,
Carried forth on wings of night.

Wrapped in stillness, time is ours,
Among the soft, twinkling stars.
Each heartbeat echoes, pure and bright,
In moments wrapped, we find our light.

The Beauty of Serene Spaces

Mountains rise with quiet grace,
Nature holds a sacred space.
In every corner, calm resides,
A tranquil heart where joy abides.

Lakes reflect the azure sky,
Whispers of the wind drift by.
In the forest, shadows play,
Nature beckons, come and stay.

Peaceful meadows stretch so wide,
Where dreams and reality coincide.
Every flower speaks its truth,
An ode to life, a song of youth.

In golden fields, the tall grass sways,
As sunlight weaves through endless days.
The beauty found in simple space,
Is a gentle and warm embrace.

In quiet moments, laughter flows,
In serene spaces, love just grows.
Amidst the stillness, hearts discern,
The beauty of life, a sweet return.

Stillness Amidst the Chaos

In the storm, a calm prevails,
A lighthouse guiding as it sails.
In swirling winds, a center found,
A quiet heart where peace is crowned.

Amid the rush, a steady breath,
Holds the line 'tween life and death.
For in chaos, stillness gleams,
A hidden whisper, woven dreams.

Like ripples on a troubled sea,
Finding solace, just to be.
In bustling streets where voices clash,
A moment's grace, an unseen splash.

Each heartbeat thunders, yet it knows,
Amidst the storm, the stillness grows.
In focused thoughts, we find our muse,
A melody we can't refuse.

So in the fray, find your retreat,
In stillness, life is bittersweet.
With open arms, embrace the night,
Where chaos fades and hearts take flight.

The Weight of Absence

In the quiet of the night,
I feel the echoing void.
Stars flicker like lost dreams,
In shadows once enjoyed.

Every whisper calls your name,
In halls that hold your grace.
Yet silence fills the space,
Where laughter left its flame.

Memories cling like soft mist,
Veiled in a tender sigh.
Each moment now dismissed,
As time drifts quietly by.

I search for warmth in dreams,
Yet find a chilling breeze.
The heart silently screams,
Longing for sweet reprieve.

Your absence writes a song,
A tune of aching bliss.
In the stillness, I belong,
Where love is framed in kiss.

This Gentle Interlude

Softly falls the evening light,
As day gives way to night.
A hush wraps 'round the trees,
In whispers on the breeze.

Time stretches like a string,
Pulled taut yet gently beckoning.
The world slows down its pace,
In this serene embrace.

Sparrows sing their final song,
As shadows dance along.
Each moment feels so rare,
Floating softly in the air.

The stars begin to peek,
Adorning velvet skies.
In this calm, we find our peak,
A stillness that unbinds.

Here lies a perfect pause,
A breath of soul's delight.
In this gentle interlude,
We savor the quiet night.

A Symphony of Shadows

In twilight's soft embrace,
Shadows weave and glide.
Silent stories find their place,
In the dimness, they bide.

Every corner holds a tale,
Of whispers, faint but clear.
As night begins to unveil,
Dreams flicker, drawing near.

The rustle of the leaves,
Plays a tune of the night.
In starlit webs, weaves,
A symphony of light.

Echoes dance on moonlit paths,
Drifting on a breeze.
In the heart, a gentle laugh,
Invites the soul to ease.

Each shadow has its grace,
In the quiet they sway.
Together, we embrace,
The magic of the gray.

Whispers of Stillness

Within the quiet dawn,
Awakens every sigh.
The world, a canvas drawn,
In hues that softly lie.

Mist hugs the waking ground,
While shadows start to fade.
In this peace, I am found,
In moments carefully laid.

Birds weave songs of bright cheer,
Each note a gentle grace.
Whispers of stillness near,
In nature's warm embrace.

Wisps of thought float and roam,
Like leaves in rivers flow.
In stillness, I find home,
Where all my worries go.

Time flows like whispered streams,
In waves of soft delight.
Here, I cradle my dreams,
In whispers of the night.

The Shape of Absence

In shadows deep, a silence grows,
Whispers linger where nobody goes.
Memories haunt the empty space,
Echoes of time, a phantom trace.

Ghostly figures flicker dim,
Fleeting thoughts on a fragile whim.
Life once vibrant, now a sigh,
In the void, our hopes still lie.

The air is thick with unlaid fare,
Every heartbeat still in the air.
Sketches of laughter, fading light,
The shape of absence haunts the night.

Yet in the darkness, a spark may gleam,
A glimmer found in a distant dream.
For even voids can hold a song,
In emptiness, we may belong.

So let us drift like whispers soft,
In the space where love takes off.
For absence shapes what we hold dear,
In the silence, you still are near.

Featherlight Dreams

On softest wings, they take to flight,
In gentle hues, the stars ignite.
A world of wonder, calm and bright,
Featherlight dreams in the still of night.

They swirl like leaves in autumn's breeze,
Brushing by with effortless ease.
Whispers of hope, a comforting sound,
In these dreams, our solace found.

Floating softly on silver beams,
Laughter dances in moonlit streams.
In magic moments, we can roam,
In featherlight dreams, we find our home.

Though dawn may break, and shadows blend,
The heart's sweet wish shall never end.
For in each dream, a truth unfurls,
A tapestry woven of endless worlds.

So close your eyes, and drift away,
Into the night where wonders play.
Embrace the lightness, let it soar,
In featherlight dreams, we live once more.

Cradles of Peace

In valleys deep, where whispers dwell,
Time gently sings its soothing bell.
Nature cradles what hearts need,
In cradles of peace, our souls are freed.

Beneath the sky, in fields of gold,
Stories of strength and love unfold.
A tender touch from hands unknown,
In silence, warmth is softly sown.

Where rivers flow and willows sway,
Hearts find comfort at the end of day.
In every breath, a quiet choice,
To listen close and find the voice.

As stars awaken, painting the night,
Dreams arise, taking their flight.
In the stillness, troubles cease,
In every moment, we find peace.

So let us gather, hand in hand,
In nature's cradle, take a stand.
For in this realm, joy will increase,
Together we bloom in cradles of peace.

Traces of Forgotten Footsteps

In the sands of time, they softly fade,
Footprints linger where paths were laid.
Stories woven in every line,
Traces of life, once intertwined.

The echoes whisper through the trees,
Memories dance with every breeze.
Paths we walked, both near and far,
Leaving behind a fleeting scar.

Each step a story, each turn a tale,
Of moments cherished, and dreams set sail.
Yet with each passing, shadows blend,
As traces fade, we learn to mend.

In quiet corners of our mind,
We search for what we hope to find.
For even footsteps lost to night,
Can guide us back to where it's right.

So let us honor those who came,
In honoring past, we share a flame.
For traces left may one day show,
The journey's worth, the love we know.

Spaces Between Words

In every pause, a silence hides,
A world unspoken, soft and wide.
Each breath a tale, unconfined,
A dance of thoughts, intertwined.

Moments lost, yet ever near,
Whispers shared, but seldom clear.
The heart's ink writes, with gentle grace,
All that lingers in our place.

Letters float in empty air,
Secrets weave, with utmost care.
In every gap, a truth unfurled,
A bridge between our joined worlds.

With every sigh, a meaning drawn,
In twilight's glow, the light is wan.
We find our voices in these breaks,
A symphony that silence makes.

So let us linger, pause, and stay,
In spaces where our hearts can play.
For in the hush, potential stirs,
In every pause, the soul confer.

The Secret Life of Shadows

In twilight's grasp, they softly creep,
A dance of forms, where secrets seep.
With silent grace, they glide and sway,
In corners where the lost souls play.

Beneath the moon, they weave a tale,
Of dreams and wishes, soft and frail.
They hold the whispers of the night,
In every flicker, hidden light.

They mold the fears we try to shun,
And flicker out when dawn's begun.
In softness cloaked, they ask for trust,
For every shadow hides its lust.

In quiet corners, they abide,
A testament to what we've tried.
Seek not to fear what they may bring,
For shadows dance, and softly sing.

So, close your eyes and see them play,
In mystery, they find their way.
Embrace their secrets, let them be,
The shadows whisper, silently.

Echoes in the Void

In silence deep, where shadows dwell,
The echoes ring of tales to tell.
In boundless space, we search for light,
But find instead the endless night.

Each thought resounds, a distant call,
In empty halls, where dreams enthrall.
The whispers fade but still await,
In every beat, we hesitate.

In vastness, time begins to fold,
A tapestry of dark and gold.
The void, a canvas, stark and bare,
Reflects our hopes, our deep despair.

Yet in this space, a promise gleams,
A flicker born from broken dreams.
For echoes carry what cannot stay,
In timeless dance, they find their way.

So listen close, to every sound,
In void and hush, our truths are found.
For in the echoes, life's refrain,
In darkness deep, we rise again.

The Stillness of the Soul's Shelter

In quietude, the spirit breathes,
Wrapped in solace that it weaves.
A sanctuary, safe and warm,
Where gentle thoughts can take their form.

Within these walls, the world recedes,
As sunlight falls like whispered seeds.
Each moment held, a treasure rare,
In stillness, burdens seem to share.

The heart finds rest, the mind takes flight,
In sacred space, a dance of light.
With every pulse, the essence flows,
In tranquil pools, the spirit knows.

So close your eyes, let silence reign,
In stillness find what cannot wane.
The soul's shelter, a waiting friend,
In quiet grace, we learn to mend.

Here in the calm, we come alive,
In inner depths, where dreams can thrive.
Embrace the peace, let chaos fade,
In stillness, beauty is remade.

When Time Takes a Breath

In the quiet hours of night,
Moments linger, softly bright.
Each tick a gentle sigh,
As stars flicker in the sky.

Time suspends its hurried race,
In this still and sacred space.
Whispers dance on cooling air,
A fleeting touch, a tender care.

Shadows stretch across the ground,
In solace, peace is found.
The world holds its breath, aligns,
In harmony, all time entwines.

Dreams drift like clouds at sea,
In this pause, we are free.
The heart beats in soft refrain,
Life's essence, without the strain.

So let the clock slow its hand,
In this moment, understand.
There is beauty in the wait,
As time breathes, we contemplate.

Reflections in a Silent Pool

Beneath the surface calm and clear,
What secrets lie, what truths appear?
The mirror of the tranquil brook,
Reveals the world, if we just look.

Ripples dance with gentle grace,
Revealing shadows, a fleeting face.
The sky reflects in hues of blue,
Nature's canvas, ever new.

A whisper of wind, a sigh from trees,
Each leaf rustles, a soft tease.
The water holds the sky's embrace,
In every drop, a sacred space.

Time dissolves in this still light,
Moments captured, pure and bright.
In silence, thoughts begin to pool,
Life's questions answered in this school.

As I gaze, the world slips by,
Reflections speak without a lie.
In this quiet, I find my whole,
Eternal truths within my soul.

The Comfort of Gentle Absence

Where whispers fade and silence reigns,
A gentle absence eases pains.
In the quiet, hearts can mend,
A soothing balm, a faithful friend.

In shadows cast by fading light,
We find comfort in the night.
The spaces where once laughter soared,
Now hold peace, gently restored.

Though echoes linger, soft yet shy,
In solitude, we learn to fly.
Each moment apart, a chance to grow,
In stillness, we begin to know.

Absence wraps like a warm embrace,
Allows the mind to find its place.
In the hush, there's room to breathe,
To cherish what we dare believe.

For in each pause, we discover more,
The beauty found in an open door.
The heart learns to dance in the still,
In gentle absence, we find our will.

Uncharted Landscapes of Stillness

Beyond the noise of everyday,
Lie lands where thoughts can drift away.
In valleys deep, where silence reigns,
Uncharted paths, the spirit gains.

Mountains rise with ancient grace,
Guarding secrets in their space.
The air is thick with quiet song,
In these realms, we all belong.

Footsteps light on mossy ground,
In every stillness, truth is found.
Nature's canvas, vast and wide,
Invites the soul to gently glide.

The sky stretches, a celestial scroll,
In its expanse, we find our role.
Each moment here, a breath embraced,
In stillness, lost time is replaced.

So wander forth, embrace the calm,
Let every heartbeat be a balm.
In uncharted lands, we uncover
The peace that whispers, always hover.

Dreams in the Dim

In shadows soft and low,
Whispers of night take flight.
Visions blend and flow,
Cradled in the gentle light.

Stars flicker, secrets shared,
Hopes that dance in cloudy skies.
Dreams are woven, unprepared,
Here in slumber, freedom lies.

Between the silence, we find,
Paths that lead to realms unknown.
Hearts and thoughts, intertwined,
In the dark, we are alone.

Fleeting moments drift and fade,
As dawn breaks on the coldest ground.
In a world where dreams are made,
We awaken, lost and found.

With every breath, a wish is spun,
A tapestry of night and day.
In dreams, we chase the sun,
Only to let it slip away.

Threads of Tranquility

In the silence of the morn,
Gentle breezes weave and sway.
Nature's lullaby is born,
Softly guiding time away.

Ripples on a placid lake,
Mirror reflections in the mist.
Each heartbeat, a calm remake,
In the stillness, peace exists.

Beneath the branches gently sway,
Time seems to pause and sigh.
Sunlight dances in the gray,
Through the leaves, it whispers why.

Clouds roll by like fleeting dreams,
Painting stories in the sky.
In this dance, the spirit beams,
Finding solace as it flies.

With each breath, we draw in ease,
Threads of calm entwine our fate.
In this moment, hearts appease,
Life unveils what love creates.

A Pause in the Chaos

In the whirl of life's embrace,
Time halts, a gentle pause.
Amidst the rush, we find our place,
Taking breath without a cause.

Chaos swirls, but here we stand,
Grounded in the present's glow.
With open hearts, we understand,
Moments lost can still bestow.

Whispers linger in the air,
Truths unravel as we wait.
Life's a tapestry to share,
Embracing love, we cultivate.

As silence wraps its arms around,
We breathe deep, let worries roam.
In this calm, we are found,
Together, we are home.

Though storms may rise, we stay awhile,
Finding joy in stillness near.
With a single, knowing smile,
We reclaim all that we hold dear.

Echoes of Forgotten Moments

In dusty corners of my mind,
Whispers call from long ago.
Fleeting shadows, truths unlined,
Painted memories that glow.

Images of laughter chase,
Faint reminders of the past.
Every smile, a warm embrace,
In the echoes, love was cast.

Time like water flows away,
Yet I cling to what once was.
Every heartache, every play,
Nestles softly, without cause.

Through the veil of yesteryear,
I find fragments of our song.
In the silence, crystal clear,
Together is where we belong.

Though the past may fade in time,
Its essence never leaves the heart.
In forgotten moments, we climb,
Reaching for a brand-new start.

The Canvas of Inactivity

In stillness, dreams reside,
Where whispers softly glide,
The clock ticks slow and light,
A world wrapped in quiet night.

Beneath the weight of time,
Life pauses, feels sublime,
Colors fade, yet do not cease,
In silence, we find peace.

A canvas stretched, no brush so bold,
Stories left untold,
Embracing shadows, nights so deep,
In inaction, secrets sleep.

Petals fall without a sound,
Timeless echoes all around,
Nature rests, her breath so sweet,
In stillness, we feel complete.

Moments lost, yet never gone,
In quietude, we carry on,
Each heartbeat writes its part,
Inactivity shades the heart.

Song of the Hidden Heart

Silent songs and whispered dreams,
Beneath the moonlight's gleams,
A melody without a name,
Flows softly, like a flame.

In shadows, secrets sway,
Tender feelings yearn to play,
Echoes of a beating drum,
Whispers tell where love may come.

Hope glimmers in the dark,
Each note, a whispered spark,
A symphony of what may be,
In silence, hearts find harmony.

Through longing's threaded line,
Passion's pulse intertwines,
A hidden song, so bittersweet,
Awakens dreams that can't retreat.

Lift the veil; hear the sound,
In stillness, love is found,
A heart's quiet symphony,
Plays on through eternity.

Envelopes of Calm

Wrapped in a gentle sigh,
Where worries drift and die,
Envelopes of serene grace,
Hold the world in a warm embrace.

Soft shadows dapple the ground,
In silence, peace is found,
As breezes whisper low,
All the chaos lays below.

Nestled in a tranquil space,
Time unfolds at its own pace,
Each breath a conscious choice,
In quietude, we find our voice.

Petals float on lazy streams,
Mirroring our silent dreams,
Water's rhythm, slow and kind,
Wraps the heart and calms the mind.

In the stillness of the night,
Stars above burn soft and bright,
Wrapped in calm, the spirit soars,
Envelopes of peace restore.

Tranquil Pathways

Winding ways through leafy green,
Nature's grace, so serene,
Footsteps on a gentle trail,
In silence, hearts prevail.

Soft whispers in the breeze,
Carry tales with gentle ease,
Where the sunlight gently plays,
Guiding us through tranquil days.

Each turn reveals a scene so grand,
In the stillness, we understand,
The beauty found in every stride,
On tranquil pathways, we confide.

Mossy stones and rustling leaves,
Nature's gift, a heart that believes,
Through quiet woods, our spirits roam,
In peace, we find our way back home.

With every step, a softened heart,
In tranquil bliss, we play our part,
The journey flows, a gentle art,
On pathways where our dreams impart.

Echoes Beneath the Surface

Whispers dance where waters meet,
Reflections hold what eyes can't see.
Secrets flow in currents sweet,
Echoes cease, but will not flee.

Ripples shatter silent dreams,
Beneath the waves, the stories weave.
Each drop glimmers, or so it seems,
Nature's heart, we dare believe.

In tranquil depths, the echoes call,
Voices lost, yet ever near.
Time stands still, it feels so small,
Beneath the surface, all is clear.

Glimmers flash like fleeting light,
Cascades of thoughts in fluid grace.
A hidden world, out of sight,
Embraces each soft, gentle trace.

In the hush, a truth confined,
Where silence breathes, and dreams awake.
Echoes loud, yet still enshrined,
In every wave, a path we take.

Solitude's Embrace

Alone beneath a starlit sky,
The quiet speaks in gentle tones.
In shadows deep, my thoughts comply,
A solace found where silence roams.

Time meanders, slow and pure,
Each moment cherished, fleeting bliss.
Wrapped in thoughts, I feel secure,
In solitude, I find my kiss.

The whisper of the midnight breeze,
Carries secrets of the night.
In stillness, I find my ease,
A world untouched, a soul's delight.

Every star, a tale to tell,
Each one a flicker of a dream.
In this darkness, all is well,
Boundless space wraps me in gleam.

So here I sit, with heart laid bare,
In solitude, where I belong.
Embraced by night, without a care,
In this stillness, hope is strong.

Shadows of Serenity

Beneath the trees where shadows play,
A tranquil world begins to breathe.
Whispers float, and drift away,
As time weaves dreams with gentle ease.

Soft rays filter through the leaves,
Dancing light on paths unshown.
In this realm, the spirit cleaves,
To nature's heart, no longer alone.

Moments wrapped in twilight grace,
Echoes of a day gone by.
In this stillness, I find my place,
With every sigh, beneath the sky.

Petals drop like feathered thoughts,
Scattering dreams upon the ground.
In sacred silence, peace is sought,
Where healing light and hope abound.

The shadows lengthen, softly sway,
Inviting me to linger near.
In nature's arms, I wish to stay,
Embraced by shadows, free of fear.

Murmurs at Twilight

As day surrenders to the night,
Murmurs linger, soft and low.
With fading light, the world takes flight,
Whispers echo where flowers grow.

The sky blazes in hues of fire,
Painting dreams with daring strokes.
In twilight's dance, we find desire,
As night unveils its timeless cloaks.

Crickets sing a serenade,
Each note a promise, sweet and clear.
In twilight's kiss, our fears do fade,
As whispers brush against the sheer.

Stars emerge like diamonds bright,
Scattered gems in velvet blue.
In fleeting moments, pure delight,
The murmurs weave a tale anew.

So here we stand, hands intertwined,
Bathed in glow of dusky charm.
In every sound, our hearts aligned,
Murmurs binding, safe and warm.

Silence Between the Beats

Time drifts slowly, hush in air,
Moments linger, a quiet prayer.
In the stillness, echoes dance,
Whispers of thoughts in a fleeting glance.

Heartbeats pause, the world is brief,
In the silence, find your chief.
Notes of calm in twilight's glow,
Between each breath, soft melodies flow.

Stillness cradles the vibrant pulse,
In the void, emotions convulse.
Lessons learned in the quiet's embrace,
Finding solace in this gentle space.

The night's curtain, gracefully drawn,
Hides the secrets of the dawn.
When words fail, let silence speak,
In the stillness, find the weak.

Between the beats, life reveals,
Hidden truths that time conceals.
Listen closely, the heart will sway,
In silence, find your way.

The Calm After the Storm

Raindrops trickle, soft and light,
Daybreak breaks, a wondrous sight.
Clouds retreat, the sun will gleam,
Peace emerges from nature's dream.

Fallen leaves in puddles lay,
Nature's rhythm finds its way.
Fresh scents rise from soaked ground,
In tranquility, joy is found.

Whispers carry on the breeze,
Gentle melodies through the trees.
Hearts once weary, now unwind,
Lost in thoughts of the divine.

The world awakens, colors bloom,
Life reclaims its rightful room.
Every sigh, a sweet release,
In soft moments, we find peace.

Together as one, we breathe anew,
In the calm, our spirits grew.
After storms, the light will beam,
Hope resides in every dream.

Soft Footfalls in the Night

Moonlight dances on quiet streets,
Shadows gather, a calm retreat.
Whispers echo with gentle stride,
Under stars, all fears subside.

Each footfall soft, a stealthy glide,
Carried by winds, we gently ride.
Nighttime's cloak, a soothing veil,
In the darkness, our dreams set sail.

Every rustle, the heart takes heed,
Nature's tales, woven seed.
Silent wonders, the world asleep,
Secrets hidden, promises keep.

In the stillness, time stands still,
Moments weave a quiet thrill.
Soft footfalls, a sacred tone,
In the night, we're never alone.

Let night's magic gently unfold,
A mystery waiting to be told.
Underneath the vast expanse,
Soft footfalls lead us to chance.

Unspoken Words of the Heart

In silence lies what hearts conceal,
Feelings deep, they long to heal.
Words unspoken hang in air,
A fragile truth, a timid flare.

Glimpses shared through fleeting gaze,
Hidden tales, a silent maze.
Every touch, electric spark,
Promises written in the dark.

Voices tremble, the fear of loss,
Bridges built but never crossed.
What we feel can't find the light,
Caught in shadows, lost from sight.

Yet in the depths of unexpressed,
Lies a love that beats in quest.
Every moment, a chance to part,
Unspoken words of the heart.

Beneath the surface, emotions swell,
Tales of longing left to tell.
In the stillness, let courage start,
To voice the whispers of the heart.

Mapping the Silent Journey

In whispers upon the winding path,
Footsteps trace the tales of old,
Silent echoes of a gentle laugh,
Stars above, a map of gold.

Through valleys deep and hills so steep,
The heart finds its way to roam,
In dreams where hidden secrets sleep,
Each turn a promise of home.

Mist dances lightly on the ground,
As shadows play among the trees,
The sound of silence, pure and profound,
Carried softly on the breeze.

With every step, a story grows,
In every pause, a breath to take,
The journey whispers, gently flows,
In nature's arms, awake, awake!

So let us chart this journey fine,
In the quiet where hearts align,
Through the stillness, love will bind,
In silent journeys, we shall shine.

Caress of the Invisible

A touch that dances on the skin,
The breath of wind, a lover's sigh,
In every pause, a subtle spin,
Invisible threads that weave and tie.

Moments linger, soft and sweet,
Like petals brushed against the face,
In the quiet, time's gentle beat,
Creates a world, a sacred space.

The warmth of thoughts yet unshared,
Hums a tune in tender air,
Cloaked in silence, souls laid bare,
In an embrace, beyond compare.

Each heartbeat echoes in the still,
The caress of the unseen touch,
In that moment, hearts can fill,
Drifting softly, ever so much.

So let us linger in the haze,
Savoring what we cannot see,
For in the invisible's gaze,
Love is an unbroken decree.

Notes of a Soft Serenade

A melody whispers through the night,
Soft and gentle, like a dream,
Each note a flicker, pure delight,
Flowing softly, a tranquil stream.

Underneath the silver moon,
Strings are plucked with tender care,
As nature hums a heartfelt tune,
Together, they craft love in air.

The rustling leaves join in the song,
Birds flare bright in harmony,
In the quiet, where we belong,
Music dances, wild and free.

With every chord, a memory made,
In the twilight where shadows play,
A serenade that will not fade,
In our hearts, it finds its way.

So let the notes of love resound,
Bright and bold against the dark,
In this soft serenade, we're bound,
A lasting glow, a vibrant spark.

Shadows Dance in Stillness

In twilight's hush, shadows draw near,
Whispers of the night unfold,
A dance in silence, sharp yet clear,
Stories in the dark retold.

Figures move with gentle grace,
Flickering in the fading light,
They weave a tapestry, embrace,
Of fleeting dreams that take their flight.

The stillness hums with ancient lore,
While echoes ripple through the air,
In this quiet, we explore,
The hidden truths that softly dare.

Each silhouette a tale of old,
Bearing witness to the time,
In their dance, the past unfolds,
To a rhythm, soft as rhyme.

So let us join this silent trance,
As shadows sway beneath the stars,
In this moment, take a chance,
And feel the magic, soft as scars.

Shadows Woven in Time

In the quiet dusk, whispers fall,
Shadows dance and silently call.
Time's embrace holds secrets deep,
Memories linger, and softly creep.

Echoes of laughter, a fleeting glance,
In twilight's glow, they spin and prance.
Moments captured in twilight's veil,
Stories woven, like a ship's sail.

Beneath the stars, the night unfolds,
Tales of the past in silence told.
The fabric of hours, stitched with care,
In shadows deep, life finds its share.

A tapestry made from stolen hours,
Fragrant blooms and faded flowers.
Life moves on, yet still remains,
In shadows, joy and sorrow reigns.

So dance with time, let moments sway,
In woven shadows, find your way.
For in their depths, the heart will see,
The beauty held in time's decree.

Conversations With the Never

In the stillness of the night,
Voices linger, lost from sight.
Every breath a silent plea,
Conversations wrapped in mystery.

Dreams whisper in the dark,
Fleeting echoes, a distant spark.
Words unspoken, held so tight,
In the realm between wrong and right.

Thoughts drift like clouds on high,
Searching for the endless sky.
In shadows deep, thoughts intertwine,
Speaking softly, yet divine.

Every moment, a chance to pause,
In the quiet, without cause.
Time evaporates, lost forever,
In this dance, we seek the never.

So listen close, as silence hums,
In conversations where stillness thrums.
The heart knows truths that often stray,
In realms of never, we find our way.

Threads of Gentle Respite

In the quiet fold of the day,
Soft threads of peace weave and sway.
Gentle moments, calm and bright,
Cradle the weary heart tonight.

With every breath, the world stands still,
Time pauses, love begins to fill.
In soft embraces, whispered tunes,
Serenity blooms beneath the moons.

Tangled worries slowly unwind,
In gentle hands, solace we find.
Each thread a story, stitched with care,
Life's tapestry, beautifully rare.

Moments shared with laughter pure,
In the softest light, we feel secure.
Together we rise, together we fall,
In threads of respite, we find it all.

So close your eyes and let it be,
In this gentle peace, we can see.
Life's rivers flow, with love's caress,
In threads of respite, we are blessed.

Meditations on Moonlight

Underneath the silver glow,
The moon whispers secrets low.
Each ray a thought, soft and clear,
In moonlit dreams, I hold you near.

Waves of light on tranquil seas,
Carried softly by the breeze.
Gentle reflections, a dance divine,
In the silence, stars align.

With every pulse, the night awakes,
A symphony of quiet aches.
Moonlight drapes the world in grace,
As shadows weave, we find our place.

In thoughts that wander through the night,
Searching for the warmth of light.
Meditations on what we crave,
In moon's embrace, our souls are brave.

So let us pause, and simply be,
In moonlit calm, we find the key.
For in this glow, our dreams take flight,
In meditations deep, all feels right.

A Veil of Tranquility

In the hush of dawn, whispers play,
Gentle breezes, softly sway,
Morning mist, a tender shroud,
Nature's peace, a quiet crowd.

The sun peeks through, a golden ray,
Birds take flight, in choreographed ballet,
Lush green leaves, dance with delight,
Tranquility flows, in purest light.

A brook meanders, with soothing sound,
Over stones and roots, it's unbound,
Reflections shimmer, a dreamlike state,
In this moment, hesitate not, but wait.

Clouds drift lazily, across the blue,
Each one a secret, a story anew,
The world's noise fades, a distant call,
In tranquility's veil, we find it all.

Time stands still, as shadows play,
In this embrace, we choose to stay,
With hearts in tune, we draw near,
In a veil of peace, we disappear.

The Essence of Nothingness

In the depths of silence lies,
A void where all existence dies,
An empty space, both vast and deep,
Where shadows linger, secrets keep.

Thoughts dissolve like morning dew,
A fleeting glance, a fading hue,
The weight of being slips away,
In nothingness, we softly sway.

A gentle whisper, a breath so light,
Embracing darkness, absorbing night,
In this realm, no fear or pain,
Just the essence, the quiet gain.

Time unravels, a thread so fine,
Each moment blends, becomes divine,
We float in peace, our souls unchained,
In the essence of void, we are explained.

A dance of thoughts, then void of sound,
The nothingness, so profound,
In the heart of silence, clarity's found,
In that essence, we are all unbound.

Shadows that Whisper

Beneath the trees, where shadows play,
Whispers linger, dance, then sway,
Each muted tone, a tale untold,
In twilight's arms, the secrets unfold.

The moonlight drapes a silken veil,
Softly urging, we follow the trail,
With every step, echoes ignite,
Revealing truths hidden from sight.

Murmurs blend with the cool night air,
Guiding us gently, a silent prayer,
In the stillness, we start to hear,
The shadows breathe, they draw us near.

Winds carry whispers from far and wide,
In every rustle, in every stride,
A chorus sings, both low and high,
In shadows, our hopes learn to fly.

Awake in dreams, the night does weave,
With each shadow, a story to believe,
Together we journey, hand in hand,
In the whispers of shadows, we stand.

The Unraveling of Sound

In the cascade where echoes dwell,
Notes converge, a fragile spell,
Whispers ripple, gentle and low,
In a twilight's grasp, they ebb and flow.

Drums of the heart begin to beat,
In syncopation, a rhythmic treat,
Melodies twine in soft embrace,
As silence dances with grace.

Strings vibrate with electric fire,
In harmony's song, we find desire,
A symphony born from quiet's womb,
In every note, a world in bloom.

The swell of sound, like ocean waves,
Carrying dreams, the music saves,
In each crescendo, we lose control,
Unraveling sound, it stirs the soul.

When the last note fades into the night,
We gather echoes, hold them tight,
For in the silence left behind,
The unraveling of sound, we find.

A Solitary Waltz

In shadows deep, I glide alone,
The moonlight casts a whispered tone.
Each step a story, soft and light,
Dancing with dreams that fade from sight.

The clock ticks slow, the world stands still,
A rhythm caught, a heart to fill.
In solitude, I find my grace,
Embracing time in this sacred space.

The stars above, they softly sway,
Guiding my feet along the way.
For in this waltz, I feel alive,
A fleeting moment, I will strive.

With every turn, I lose my fears,
Echoes linger, stilled by years.
In twilight's embrace, I find my song,
A solitary dance, where I belong.

So let the night wrap me in dreams,
Where silence flows and moonlight gleams.
In this tender waltz, I am free,
Just shadows and a memory.

Traces of a Whisper

In tangled thoughts, a whisper stirs,
Like distant echoes, soft and blurred.
It weaves through time, yet lingers near,
A gentle breath, a silent cheer.

Traces of words upon the breeze,
Caressing leaves on ancient trees.
A hint of laughter, a shade of light,
Binding the day to the velvet night.

Each moment passes, yet still it stays,
In fading twilight, soft and haze.
Memories linger, like morning dew,
Painting the world in shades anew.

Whispers of love, they kiss the air,
Reminding hearts of joy and care.
In every silence, a story told,
The warmth of spirits, brave and bold.

So let these whispers dance and twine,
In the heart's rhythm, a sweet design.
For in these traces, we find our place,
A tapestry woven with tender grace.

Dusk's Quiet Canvas

As day surrenders to evening's glow,
The sky transforms with a gentle flow.
Brushstrokes of orange, pink, and grey,
Canvas of silence, fading away.

Each moment drips like painted light,
Colors blending in the soft twilight.
Birds settle down in their hidden nests,
Nature's hush brings tranquil rests.

The shadows dance as stars appear,
Whispers of night that draw us near.
A quiet beauty that speaks so clear,
In dusk's embrace, all doubt may disappear.

The world slows down, bathed in peace,
Hopes and dreams take flight, release.
Each breath a sigh, each heart a beat,
On dusk's canvas, life feels complete.

So let the colors weave and swirl,
In every heart, a secret pearl.
For in the stillness, magic thrives,
In dusk's embrace, our spirit strives.

Still Waves of Emotion

In a quiet cove, the waters rest,
Whispers of feelings within the chest.
Each ripple speaks of love and pain,
Still waves carry their soft refrain.

The tides of time ebb and flow,
Memories stir in the undertow.
Each wave a heartbeat, rising high,
Beneath the surface, dreams do lie.

In silence deep, the ocean sighs,
Reflecting hopes, unspoken cries.
A gentle touch from the hand of fate,
Guiding our souls to navigate.

Still waves glisten under the moon,
A tender light that speaks too soon.
For in emotion, we find our truth,
A boundless sea, eternal youth.

So let the waves of feeling swell,
Carrying stories we cannot tell.
In each gentle lap against the shore,
The heart knows love forevermore.

Where Noise Fades

In quiet corners shadows play,
Whispers dance where thoughts decay.
The rush of life begins to stall,
In gentle moments, silence calls.

Beneath the stars, the stillness grows,
A balm for all that life bestows.
With every breath, the chaos wanes,
In tranquil hearts, peace ever reigns.

Time drifts softly, like a stream,
In midnight's grasp, we dare to dream.
Where noise once roared, now calm pervades,
In the embrace, where noise fades.

Leaves rustle lightly, secrets shared,
In nature's song, we've all repaired.
Here in the hush, we find our way,
With every heartbeat, night turns to day.

So heed the quiet, let it be,
In silence, find your constancy.
A world transformed, a gentle trade,
In the soft sphere where noise fades.

Lullaby of the Evening

The sun dips low, its colors blend,
A calming grace, the day's sweet end.
Crickets sing in soft refrain,
Their melodies wash away the pain.

The breeze, a whisper, wraps around,
As twilight's cloak blankets the ground.
Stars awaken, one by one,
Each spark a promise, softly spun.

In this hush, the heart can rest,
Each sigh a prayer, a gentle quest.
Beneath the moon's soft guiding light,
The world transforms, bids us goodnight.

Dreams take flight on wings of hope,
In night's embrace, we learn to cope.
The lullaby of the evening sings,
Of tranquil nights and hopeful things.

So close your eyes, embrace the night,
In peaceful dreams, find pure delight.
The lullaby, a gentle call,
In midnight's grip, we find our all.

Sighs of the Soul

In the quiet, secrets weave,
The heart speaks truths we dare not leave.
Each sigh a story deep within,
A tale of battles lost and won.

Silent echoes of the past,
In every corner, shadows cast.
The weight of dreams, the light of hope,
In sighs we learn, we grieve, we cope.

Whispers linger in the air,
Tender moments stripped bare.
The soul's lament, a soft refrain,
In every heartbeat, love and pain.

With every breath, a truth unfolds,
In sighs of silver, tales of gold.
Each tear a testament of grace,
In every sigh, a warm embrace.

So let them flow, these anguished notes,
In sighs, the soul's own heartbeat floats.
A symphony of loss and gain,
In every sigh, we break the chain.

The Unspoken Language

In glances shared and quiet smiles,
A world beyond, yet close by miles.
With every breath, unvoiced we meet,
In silence stretched, the heart's own beat.

Hands brush lightly, a fleeting touch,
Words unneeded, we feel so much.
In the space where thoughts align,
The unspoken blooms, a sacred sign.

Eyes like candles, flicker, gleam,
In the hush, we weave our dream.
Each heartbeat speaks a story clear,
In the stillness, we draw near.

Time bends softly, moments blend,
In this language, no need to pretend.
The world falls silent, we comprehend,
In every glance, our souls transcend.

So let us cherish this sweet refrain,
In the unspoken, find love's domain.
A bond unbroken, rich and true,
In silence, I speak, I see you.

Cradle of the Mute

A whisper hangs in twilight air,
Where silence rocks a tender care.
Dreams drift gently, soft and wide,
In the arms where secrets hide.

Stars blink softly, a lullaby,
Underneath the vast night sky.
Cradles hold what words can't say,
In the hush of fading day.

Eyes closed tight, a peaceful sigh,
Veils of night like clouds drift by.
Stillness wraps the world around,
In the quiet, love is found.

Echoes whisper, soft and sweet,
In the silence, hearts will meet.
Cradle this, the unspoken bond,
In the still, where we respond.

Time stands still, in shadows cast,
Though the moments flee so fast.
Here we linger, souls entwined,
In the hush, our dreams aligned.

Murmurs of the Heart

Beneath the surface, soft and deep,
Where secrets dwell, we dare to leap.
Murmurs rising, sweet and low,
In the quiet, feelings flow.

Gentle pulses, tender beats,
In the silence, love entreats.
Fingers brushing, sparks ignite,
In the dusk, our hearts take flight.

Voices blend in whispered song,
In this place where we belong.
Every look, a story spun,
In the shadows, we are one.

Time slows down, the world fades out,
In your eyes, I feel no doubt.
Murmurs echo, soft and clear,
In this moment, I am near.

Nature sings, the night so bright,
In these murmurs, pure delight.
Hold this, every fleeting part,
In the whispers of the heart.

Breath of the Undisturbed

In the stillness, nature breathes,
Cradled deep beneath the leaves.
Every rustle, every sigh,
Marks the passage of the sky.

Gentle winds weave through the trees,
Whispers carried on the breeze.
Time stands still, the world at peace,
In this moment, sweet release.

Rippling waters, soft and clear,
Reflect the calm that gathers here.
Footsteps fall on cushioned ground,
In the silence, solace found.

Nature's hymn, a quiet song,
Where the heart beats, wild and strong.
Breath of life, untouched and pure,
In this stillness, we endure.

Stars above, a watchful eye,
In this breath, we dare to fly.
Every heartbeat, every prayer,
In the peace, we find our care.

Shadows in Soft Light

Shadows dance in the golden glow,
Where the light begins to slow.
Fading hues, a soft embrace,
Whispered tales in a hidden space.

Leaves flutter, a gentle sigh,
Caught between the earth and sky.
Moments linger, softly blurred,
In this light, no need for words.

Time drifts on, the world remote,
In the shadows, dreams will float.
Every shimmer tells a tale,
In the soft light, we prevail.

Footsteps soft on winding paths,
In the quiet, love still laughs.
Merging dusk with dawn's sweet call,
In the shadows, we'll not fall.

Breath of twilight wraps the land,
Fingers touch, a sacred hand.
In this realm, we find our way,
In the shadows, light will stay.

The Hush of Dawn

In gentle light, the world awakes,
Whispers of day, the silence breaks.
Birds begin their morning song,
A soft reminder, we belong.

The mist that clings to every tree,
A tranquil moment, wild and free.
Sunrise paints the sky in gold,
A story new, yet often told.

Shadows lengthen, then recede,
The earth unfolds its quiet creed.
In the hush, our hearts will soar,
Embrace the peace, forevermore.

Each step a promise, soft and sweet,
With nature's pulse, our hearts will meet.
In the dawn's embrace, we find our way,
To greet the hope of a new day.

So linger here in morning's glow,
Where dreams awaken, time flows slow.
In every breath, a gift profound,
Find solace in the hush of dawn.

A Lullaby of Silence

In tranquil night, the world is still,
Wrapped in shadows, calm and chill.
Stars above in silence gleam,
Whispers fold in a soothing dream.

Crickets chirp a lullaby,
While moonlight dances in the sky.
A gentle breeze, a soft caress,
Embracing peace, we find our rest.

The heart finds solace, pure and deep,
In the quietude, secrets keep.
With every sigh, the world lets go,
In silence shared, our spirits grow.

The echoes fade of day's long toil,
Nature hums, her quiet coil.
A tender night, a soft embrace,
In this silence, we find our place.

So close your eyes and drift away,
Into the night, let worries sway.
In this lullaby of night's sweet grace,
We find the strength of quiet space.

Still Waters Run Deep

Beneath the surface, secrets lie,
In stillness, truth will never die.
Reflecting skies of azure hue,
Where dreams are born, and hope anew.

The quiet depth, a calming sight,
Holds echoes softly, hearts take flight.
A mirror to the sky above,
It speaks of peace, it speaks of love.

Ripples form with every breath,
A dance of life, a dance with death.
In quiet waters, wisdom dwells,
With stories all the silence tells.

The gentleness of water flows,
Through valleys deep where no one goes.
It holds the whispers of the night,
In stillness found, we seek the light.

So linger near the water's edge,
Where thoughts arise and fears allege.
In stillness gaze upon the deep,
Where heart and mind in silence leap.

Secrets of the Hidden Hour

In twilight's hush, the world feels shy,
When day meets night, and dreams can fly.
A fleeting moment, lost in time,
Where silence sings its gentle rhyme.

The shadows weave a tale profound,
As secrets whisper all around.
In the hidden hour, truth is laid,
Where hopes are born, and fears are slayed.

The fleeting light, a soft embrace,
Invites the stars to take their place.
In dusk's caress, we lean and sway,
To listen close to what they say.

With every breath, the magic flows,
In hidden realms where wonder grows.
The beauty found in shadows near,
In moments soft, our hearts can clear.

So cherish now this sacred sphere,
Let troubles melt, let joy draw near.
In the hidden hour, find your bliss,
In whispered dreams and starlit kiss.

Whispers of Stillness

In twilight's glow, shadows creep,
Silent thoughts begin to seep,
The world slows, a gentle sigh,
As starlit dreams begin to fly.

Nature breathes, a soft refrain,
The moonlit path, the light of grain,
In every rustle, a story told,
Where whispers of stillness unfold.

A fleeting breeze, a tender touch,
A moment captured, it means so much,
In quiet corners, solace thrives,
In the stillness, life survives.

Time pauses here, beneath the trees,
Each sigh mingled with the breeze,
A canvas painted, hues so rare,
In whispers of stillness, hearts repair.

Close your eyes, let worries fade,
In the silence, love is laid,
Follow the echoes, soft and pure,
In stillness, we always endure.

Echoes of Solitude

In the heart of night, shadows play,
A silent room where dreams sway,
Lost in thoughts, drifting wide,
In echoes of solitude, I confide.

Whispers linger on the air,
A quiet space, a breath of care,
In solitude's embrace, I find,
A melody of the gentle mind.

Stars blink softly, distant and bright,
In this moment, darkness feels light,
With every heartbeat, stories stir,
In echoes of solitude, I concur.

The clock ticks slow, time stands still,
In every pause, I find my will,
In the silence, strength is found,
In echoes of solitude, I am bound.

Crickets sing their midnight song,
In solitude, I feel so strong,
A journey traveled deep within,
In echoes of solitude, I begin.

Beneath the Hush

Beneath the hush of evening light,
The world dons a cloak of night,
Every whisper seems to hum,
A tranquil heart begins to drum.

Softly breathing, stars align,
In muted breaths, the world's divine,
Each glance at stars, a story shared,
In the hush, our dreams are bared.

The moon spills silver on the ground,
In stillness, a soft peace is found,
Where shadows dance and hearts unwind,
Beneath the hush, the lost we find.

Every moment feels complete,
As time and dreams begin to meet,
In nature's hold, we're gently cradled,
Beneath the hush, our spirits fabled.

So listen close, the night will share,
A symphony woven in the air,
In quiet spaces, souls ignite,
Beneath the hush, we find our light.

Serenity's Embrace

In gentle dawn, the sun awakes,
With every ray, the silence breaks,
The world unfurls in colors bright,
In serenity's embrace, pure light.

Fields of gold and skies so blue,
A calming peace, a heart so true,
In every petal, every leaf,
In serenity's embrace, find relief.

A whisper flows through quiet streams,
In nature's heart, we chase our dreams,
With every ripple, joy's caress,
In serenity's embrace, we are blessed.

Time slows down in fragrant air,
In every pause, a moment rare,
With every breath, our spirits dance,
In serenity's embrace, we take a chance.

So close your eyes, breathe in this grace,
In every heartbeat, find your place,
In stillness deep, where love can trace,
In serenity's embrace, we find our space.

Moments of Wandering Light

In the dawn's soft glow, we wander free,
Chasing shadows beneath a rustling tree.
Sunbeams dance upon the morning dew,
Each flicker whispers secrets anew.

With each step taken, time starts to bend,
Colors twirl and in the air they blend.
Dreams float gently like leaves on the stream,
In these moments, we weave our own dream.

As dusk arrives, with stars we align,
Fleeting glimmers, in silence they shine.
Guiding us home through the velvet night,
Embracing the warmth of that wandering light.

Paths may drift, yet we follow our heart,
In this journey, we each play our part.
Lost and found in the beauty of flight,
Moments captured in wandering light.

Eternal echoes of laughter and sighs,
In each fleeting cut across the skies.
A tapestry woven from whispers of time,
Moments of magic, forever entwined.

Timelessness of Quietude

In the hush where shadows softly dwell,
Quietude wraps around like a shell.
The world outside fades, whispers take flight,
Embracing the warmth of unbroken night.

Moments stretch like shadows in the sun,
Time drips slowly, as if it has won.
Stillness whispers secrets meant to enthrall,
In that silence, we catch the soft call.

Thoughts linger gently, like dew on the grass,
In this sacred space, all worries pass.
Serenity blossoms where chaos once thrived,
In the depths of the quiet, we feel alive.

Embrace the absence of hurry or haste,
In timelessness, no moment laid to waste.
Each breath a treasure, each heartbeat divine,
In the stillness, our souls intertwine.

As night falls softly, stars gracefully peep,
In the tranquil shadows, the world is asleep.
Yet in this quiet, we find our own light,
A gathering of peace, enduring and bright.

The Weight of Nonbeing

In the void where shadows blend and fade,
Echoes whisper truths too deep to trade.
Tangled thoughts drift like clouds in the sky,
The weight of nonbeing, a solemn sigh.

Each step forward feels heavier still,
As echoes of nothingness bend to will.
Waves of silence crash upon the shore,
In the depths of absence, we seek for more.

Yet in this stillness, we find our own song,
Melodies crafted where we feel we belong.
The burden of emptiness lingers near,
Yet it is here that our hearts learn to steer.

In the depths of the void, we stretch our hands,
Finding connection in invisible strands.
In the vastness where meaning takes flight,
We embrace the weight of the soft, dense night.

With each breath taken, we dance on the edge,
Of nothingness curling like smoke on a ledge.
In the paradox, we awaken our being,
In the heart of nonbeing, we find our freeing.

Reflections in the Still Light

In the glow of dusk, mirrors unfold,
Reflections shimmer, stories untold.
A quiet lake holds dreams in its sway,
As ripples whisper secrets of the day.

Silhouettes drift in the twilight embrace,
In stillness, we find forgotten grace.
Each glance captured within the soft glow,
Chronicles of life that ebb and flow.

The colors swirl, painting tales anew,
In the soft light, the world feels askew.
Yet in this moment, clarity blooms bright,
In reflections we traverse through the night.

Time stands silent in that mirrored expanse,
Each heartbeat echoes a gentle dance.
As we gaze deeper, shadows confide,
Within the still light, our fears coincide.

Embracing the calm, we find we belong,
In the echoes of dusk, forever strong.
Reflections shimmer, guiding our sight,
Through the corridors of the still light.

Between the Lines of a Whisper

In shadows where secrets hide,
Words dance, softly side by side.
Echoes linger, gentle and light,
Unraveling tales in the night.

Here silence speaks, a tender thread,
Binding hearts to words unsaid.
Between the lines, a world unfolds,
Each silence a story, quietly told.

Through quiet breaths, and softest sighs,
Misunderstandings wear no disguise.
In whispered tones, truth finds a way,
Painting love in shades of gray.

Close your eyes, hear the refrain,
Every silence possesses a gain.
In the pause, connection ignites,
Crafting dreams on starry nights.

So linger here, within the hush,
Where the heart learns to trust.
Between the lines, life takes flight,
Whispers weave through the night.

Stillness in the Storm

Amid the chaos, calm resides,
With every wave, the heart abides.
Beneath the thunder, a quiet plea,
A yearning for peace, to simply be.

Clouds may clash with vibrant rage,
Yet stillness whispers, turns the page.
In every gust that bends the trees,
There's a solace, a gentle breeze.

Hold tight to moments, fleeting and rare,
In the storm's eye, find solace there.
Though winds may howl, and rains may fall,
The spirit stands firm, above it all.

Listen closely, the heart remains,
In the tempest, it breaks chains.
Grace finds roots in turmoil's seam,
A dance of strength, a waking dream.

So when the skies begin to roar,
Seek that stillness, forevermore.
For in that space, the heart can soar,
And storms will fade, forevermore.

The Palette of Silence

In hues of dusk, the silence grows,
A canvas blooming, no one knows.
Brushstrokes whisper, soft and bold,
Tales of longing, yet untold.

Colors blend in twilight's grace,
Giving life to an empty space.
Each pause a hue, each breath a stroke,
Captured moments, softly spoke.

Underneath the stars, it sways,
In tranquil tones, the heart conveys.
A melody crafted without sound,
In quiet corners, dreams are found.

See the beauty in what's not said,
In silent echoes, make your bed.
Paint your world with love's intent,
The palette of silence, heaven-sent.

So linger here, where shadows bloom,
In the quiet, dispel the gloom.
With every whisper of the night,
The palette glows with colors bright.

The Still Room of the Soul

In a corner of the mind's embrace,
Find a still room, a sacred space.
Where thoughts can rest and freely flow,
In the quiet, let the spirit grow.

Here shadows linger, soft and sweet,
Each moment, a heartbeat's beat.
With every sigh, the essence reveals,
Truths unspoken that time conceals.

Cherish the stillness, the gentle air,
Where burdens lighten, and love can share.
In whispered dreams, the heart unfolds,
A tapestry of stories told.

So close your eyes, and breathe it in,
Let serenity wash away the din.
In this still room, the soul finds peace,
Awakening joy, a sweet release.

Here's to the moments, quiet and bright,
In the still room, find your light.
A sanctuary deep within,
Where life begins, and love can spin.

Embracing the Void

In silence deep, where shadows creep,
I find a space, where thoughts can leap.
A dark embrace, with whispered call,
I lose myself, yet feel it all.

The weight of none, the breath of few,
In boundless dark, where dreams break through.
Each star a thought, both lost and found,
In this expanse, I'm tightly bound.

Between the worlds, the stillness sings,
A gentle pull, the void it brings.
With every pulse, a quiet fight,
In blackened depths, I seek the light.

From edges frayed, I weave my thread,
With every doubt, a path I tread.
Embracing all, the fear, the grace,
In quietude, I find my place.

So let me drift, away from sight,
Into the dark, towards the light.
For in this void, I'm ever free,
To be the soul that dares to be.

The Ghosts of Still Moments

In shadowed corners, echoes sigh,
The whispers of time float softly by.
Forgotten laughter, a lingering tune,
Ghosts of still moments, beneath the moon.

The air is thick with memories past,
A fleeting glance, too brief to last.
Softly I wander, through spaces lost,
Counting the joys, and bearing the cost.

Each breath an image, a fleeting glance,
Moments entwined in a timeless dance.
Fleeting yet steady, they wrap around,
In stillness, I hear the heart's soft sound.

With every heartbeat, the shadows play,
A symphony woven in shades of gray.
Though time eludes, I hold them tight,
The ghosts of still moments, a cherished light.

As silence lingers, my spirit sways,
In the embrace of these endless days.
For every memory that softly blooms,
A ghost of still moments, in quiet rooms.

Calming Tides of Memory

The tides of time roll in and out,
With whispers soft, they speak no doubt.
Each wave that crashes, a tale to tell,
Of love and loss, and wishing well.

In quiet shores, where dreams reside,
I find my peace, where memories guide.
Each grain of sand, a moment still,
In calming tides, my heart can fill.

The ocean breathes, with gentle grace,
A liquid mirror, my soul's embrace.
In rhythmic flow, I drift away,
With tides of memory, here I stay.

As sunsets fade, and darkness creeps,
The heart remembers, while silence sleeps.
In every ebb, in every flow,
Calming tides teach me to let go.

So I shall bask in this serenade,
With waves of time, I am remade.
For in each tide that pulls and sways,
Memory holds me, and gently stays.

Beyond the Clamor

In bustling crowds, noise fills the air,
Yet whispers linger, a breath to share.
Beyond the clamor, a secret space,
Where silence gathers, a warm embrace.

The world spins on, with hurried feet,
Yet in my heart, I find my beat.
In stillness found, amidst the storm,
A quiet refuge, a place to warm.

Each voice a note in the grand design,
But here I stand, a moment mine.
With echoes fading, I hear the call,
Beyond the clamor, I rise, I fall.

The chaos swirls like leaves in flight,
Yet here I anchor, in soft twilight.
With every breath, I choose to see,
Beyond the clamor, just me and me.

So let the world spin wild and free,
I'll carve my path, my harmony.
In whispers gentle, my spirit blooms,
Beyond the clamor, my heart resumes.

Hushed Reverie

In the stillness of the night,
Dreams take flight, whispers soft,
Twinkling stars in silent sight,
Hearts aflame, spirits aloft.

A gentle breeze caresses skin,
Echoes of laughter drift afar,
Moments stitched, where do we begin?
Time is woven into a star.

Beneath the shade of ancient trees,
Memories held in shadows dance,
Fleeting moments carried with ease,
In this hush, we find our chance.

Candles flicker like our hopes,
Casting light on dreams unsure,
In every sigh, the spirit copes,
Love's embrace, a gentle cure.

Each heartbeat echoes in the deep,
As night unfolds its velvet veil,
In this hush, we dare to leap,
Spinning tales where love prevails.

When Time Pauses

In stillness, the world holds breath,
Moments frozen in golden light,
Seconds stretch beyond all death,
Time whispers softly, taking flight.

With each glance, the universe spins,
A clock that melts in warm embrace,
Life's rhythm dances, softly wins,
A fleeting pause, a sacred space.

Through shifting sands, we find our way,
As shadows lengthen, day turns dusk,
In quietude, dreams start to play,
In echoes, memories we trust.

Hope unfurls like petals wide,
In this moment, hearts entwine,
Where silence spreads, love does abide,
A timeless spell, a tender sign.

So let us tread on velvet paths,
Where clocks forget their tireless chase,
Embrace the still, let go of wraths,
In this pause, we find our grace.

The Beauty of Low Tides

As the ocean breathes a sigh,
The shore reveals its sandy skin,
Shells and treasures left to dry,
In quietude, the waves begin.

Tides recede, unveil the past,
Secrets held beneath the waves,
Whispers of the ocean vast,
In each rise, a story saves.

Footprints linger, moments trace,
As the sun dips low and shy,
Underneath the sky's embrace,
Golden hues gracefully lie.

Nature's rhythm hums along,
A lullaby of ebb and flow,
In this space, we find our song,
In the low tides, dreams often grow.

So let us wander, hand in hand,
Write our tales upon the sand,
In the quiet, love expands,
The beauty of low tides, our land.

Secrets in Gentle Breezes

Whispers float on currents light,
A hush that greets the waking day,
Leaves sway softly, hearts take flight,
Secrets carried far away.

Through the trees, a story weaves,
Echoes of laughter in the air,
Nature sings while the spirit believes,
In the breeze, we find our care.

Clouds drift slowly, dreams align,
Carried forth on summer's breath,
In the warmth, a touch divine,
Love unspoken, a dance with death.

Each rustle holds a fleeting trace,
The past, the present intertwined,
In every gust, we find our grace,
Gentle breezes, the heart's designed.

So breathe in deep, let worries go,
In the gentle winds, we rise,
With every whisper, we shall know,
The secrets held beneath the skies.

Lament of the Unattended

In shadows deep, my whispers fade,
Unheard they drift, like dreams betrayed.
A fragile heart, left all alone,
Sings softly to the silent stone.

Each passing day, a heavy sigh,
A longing glance, a muted cry.
The echoes dance, yet none can see,
This aching soul, a memory.

Forgotten paths, where silence reigns,
A tapestry of unshared pains.
I reach for hands, but find the air,
A ghost of love, a fading prayer.

In twilight's glow, the stars align,
But still, I wait, for hearts to bind.
The night is calm, yet shadows creep,
In dreams, I stir, the truth is steep.

So here I stand, a watchful plea,
In the vast void, where none can see.
The world moves on, a distant song,
Yet here I linger, lost, and long.

Gently Falling Leaves

In autumn's breath, the colors blend,
A symphony of change, no end.
The rustling whispers through the trees,
A dance so slow, like drifting seas.

Their golden hues, a fleeting grace,
Embrace the earth, their final place.
A carpet soft, beneath my feet,
Each step a memory, bittersweet.

As twilight falls, the shadows grow,
A gentle hush, where soft winds blow.
The leaves descend, with quiet sighs,
Embodying the truth that flies.

A tapestry of time unfolds,
In swirling eddies, stories told.
They twirl and spin, a soft ballet,
Reminding us that all must sway.

The ground adorned, a scene divine,
Nature's art, in perfect design.
With each leaf fall, a note of peace,
An ode to life, a sweet release.

Secrets Beneath the Surface

Beneath the waves, the silence grows,
A hidden world, where mystery flows.
The depths conceal what's rarely seen,
A realm eternal, where shadows glean.

Coral castles, vibrant and bright,
Guard whispered tales, in the dark of night.
With every current, secrets weave,
A dance of life, so hard to believe.

The fish that glide, in colors bold,
Are storytellers of truths untold.
They twist and turn with knowing grace,
In this quiet, sacred space.

The ocean's heart, a keeper wise,
Holds ancient dreams, beneath the skies.
Each ripple speaks of joys and woes,
An echo soft, where time bestows.

So dive within, where wonders play,
And let the depths wash fears away.
For secrets kept in silent blue,
Hold keys to worlds, both old and new.

The Space Between Heartbeats

In fleeting moments, time suspends,
A breath held tight, where stillness bends.
Each heartbeat whispers soft and low,
A rhythm only silence knows.

The pause between, a sacred space,
Where dreams can linger, find their place.
A heartbeat's echo, soft and clear,
Whispers the truths we long to hear.

In tender nights, when shadows play,
The space between holds night and day.
A gentle hush, a soft embrace,
In silence, thoughts can interlace.

The world may rush, but here I stay,
In quietude, I find my way.
Each moment stretched, a canvas wide,
Where love and longing softly bide.

So let me dwell in this sweet space,
Where heartbeats dance with timeless grace.
In every pause, a life unfolds,
And whispers softly, love beholds.

The Unspoken Melody

In whispers soft the shadows hum,
A tune that calls but stays undone.
Each silence sings a gentle sound,
The heart's sweet song, forever bound.

Beneath the stars, a vision glows,
A thread of dreams no one yet knows.
The night reveals what words can't share,
A melody that fills the air.

Amongst the leaves that dance so free,
An echo of what's meant to be.
The harmony of hopes concealed,
In quiet moments, truth revealed.

With each heartbeat, a note takes flight,
Creating warmth in the cool of night.
The unsung ballad of our days,
Plays softly in so many ways.

So let the silence sing its tune,
In twilight's arms, beneath the moon.
For every note that goes unheard,
Is still a song, a whispered word.

Observing the Unknown

Through the mist, the shadows creep,
Where secrets lie and stillness sleeps.
In every glance, a tale unfolds,
In silence shared, the truth beholds.

Hidden paths where few have trod,
Guide the way to what's unshod.
Eyes wide open, hearts prepare,
To see the worlds that linger there.

Unseen faces in the crowd,
Whispers soft yet ever loud.
Each moment rich with latent light,
Admiring wonders hidden from sight.

In shadows deep, the stories swell,
Every silence has a spell.
To wander through the uncharted air,
Is to embrace the mystic rare.

So linger here where time stands still,
Let curiosity fulfill.
For in the unknown lies the key,
To paths untraveled, wild and free.

Breathing Between Thoughts

In the pauses, a space unfolds,
A quiet breath, a tale retold.
Moments lost in the rush of haste,
Echo softly, never to waste.

Between the lines, a silence waits,
Hints of meaning One cultivates.
Each heartbeat's sigh, a whispered pause,
Inviting peace, revealing cause.

As thoughts collide in vibrant streams,
Between them flows the river of dreams.
Gentle currents cradle the mind,
In stillness found, the souls aligned.

Embrace the slumber of the night,
In breath's embrace, we find the light.
For in the gaps, the heart does sing,
The beauty in the pause we bring.

So linger long in sweet refrain,
Breathe deeply in the calm of rain.
For there, within the quiet thought,
Lies the wonder life has sought.

The Beauty of Unheard Cries

In shadows cast by silent pleas,
The world can miss the aching leaves.
Unheard voices call through the night,
Hidden dreams just out of sight.

With every tear that falls in vain,
A story waits, a pulse of pain.
But in the quiet, strength does grow,
A resilience that few may know.

Among the stillness, hope is spun,
A tapestry of battles won.
In muted whispers lies the grace,
Of haunting beauty in the space.

Each cry that fades into the dark,
Is but a seed, a hidden spark.
In silence, wisdom often grows,
In unheard cries, the heart bestows.

So listen close, my dear, and find,
The beauty wrapped in life, entwined.
For every soul that feels alone,
Holds a story waiting to be known.

Whispers Among the Trees

In the woods where secrets lie,
Leaves converse beneath the sky.
Branches sway in rhythmic grace,
Nature's voice, a soft embrace.

Echoes dance in twilight's glow,
Stories shared that none will know.
Roots entwined in silent trust,
Whispers linger, fair and just.

Mossy carpets, aged and wise,
Hold the tales of time that flies.
Breezes carry hushed refrain,
Greeting peace where dreams remain.

Flickering lights on bark so grand,
Signal truths we understand.
In each rustle, life unfolds,
In these woods, our hearts consoled.

As day departs, a calm descends,
A gentle hush, the twilight bends.
Every whisper, each tender sound,
In the trees, our hopes were found.

The Pause Before Tomorrow

In the hush before the dawn,
Hope awakens, dreams are drawn.
Shadows fade, the light breaks free,
The world holds breath, as if to see.

Moments linger, time stands still,
Promises whispered against the chill.
Stars fade softly, threads of gold,
New beginnings, stories told.

A heartbeat echoes, softly near,
Carrying wishes, laced with fear.
The dawn awaits with open arms,
Embracing all the world's sweet charms.

Quiet thoughts weave through the air,
Anticipation everywhere.
Morning light, a canvas bright,
Painting dreams beyond the night.

In this pause, the future glows,
With every sunrise, love still grows.
A dance of hope, a gentle sigh,
The promise lives, we dare to fly.

Silence Between Heartbeats

In the stillness, a pulse remains,
A quiet rhythm that softly sustains.
Moments stretched like shadows long,
In the hush, we find our song.

Heartbeats whisper, soft and low,
Secrets shared that few will know.
Breath held tight, the world fades out,
Within the silence, we live, no doubt.

The space between, a tender grace,
In every pause, we find our place.
Each heartbeat echoing through time,
A gentle whisper, a silent rhyme.

Lost in thoughts, our spirits soar,
Where silence speaks and hearts explore.
A language found in teardrops bright,
A symphony born from darkest night.

In silence, love reveals its truth,
In muted tones, the pulse of youth.
In every heartbeat, stories blend,
A quiet promise, wounds will mend.

Flickers of Quietude

In twilight's glow, the world slows down,
Flickers dance above the town.
Soft whispers curl in evening air,
Fleeting moments that we share.

Stars prick through the velvet sky,
Silent wishes, dreams on high.
In the calm, we find our peace,
In this stillness, worries cease.

Every flicker, a calming light,
Guides us through the gentle night.
Shadows play on walls of thought,
In quietude, our souls are caught.

As crickets sing their lullaby,
The world exhales a sleepy sigh.
In this moment, hearts align,
Flickers of quiet, so divine.

With every breath, the night enfolds,
A tapestry of dreams retold.
Flickers fade, but hope stays bright,
In the quiet, we find our light.

Solace in the Stillness

In the hush of twilight's glow,
Whispers of peace start to flow,
Stars twinkle, soft and bright,
A tender kiss from the night.

Breath of calm fills the air,
Quiet moments, free from care,
Nature's lullaby begins,
A soothing song that always wins.

Trees sway gently in the breeze,
Time slows down, hearts find ease,
Lost in thoughts, the world fades,
Serenity in the glades.

Dreams emerge from shadows deep,
In this stillness, secrets keep,
Eyes closed, the spirit soars,
In the silence, the soul explores.

Here we find our truest selves,
Sheltered far from worldly shelves,
Moments linger, simple, sweet,
In stillness, we are complete.

Veils of Muffled Thought

Fragments of dreams weave through air,
Thoughts like whispers, almost rare,
Clad in shadows, softly veiled,
Where echoes of silence have prevailed.

Amidst the noise, a gentle hum,
Yet in this quiet, questions come,
Drifting clouds of uncertainty,
Lurking just beyond the sea.

Each layer peeled, we search for light,
In the dim, the heart takes flight,
Veils will lift, but slowly so,
Revealing paths we long to know.

In the corner of the mind,
Answers hidden, hard to find,
Hints of truth in fleeting sighs,
Greeting dawn with open eyes.

With every breath, we break the chain,
Embracing joy, releasing pain,
Veils will flutter with the breeze,
Unraveling all that seeks to please.

Serenade of the Unheard

Beneath the din of daily grind,
A melody for the blind,
Softly sung by hidden souls,
In shadows where the silence rolls.

Chords of longing float on air,
With every heartbeat, a lover's prayer,
Echoing in the empty night,
A serenade, pure and bright.

Notes that dance on the edge of dreams,
Flowing like gentle streams,
Weaving tales that time forgot,
In this realm, they burn hot.

With whispered breaths, the spirits play,
Songs of hope to light the way,
Words unspoken, truths unchained,
In the silence, love remains.

Gathered stars in soft embrace,
Signatures of unseen grace,
Melodies drift like petals fall,
An unheard balled waits for all.

Cacophony of Silence

Amidst the calm, a storm can brew,
Whispers collide, and shadows skew,
Silence speaks in riddled tones,
A symphony of subtle groans.

Layers of quiet lie compressed,
Echoes clash where dreams are pressed,
Voices tangled, lost in thought,
In the stillness, battles fought.

Thoughts like thunder in the void,
A cacophony, dreams destroyed,
Peace replaced with anxious beats,
In silence' heart, chaos greets.

Yet through this clash, a truth may rise,
A clearer view through tempest skies,
Where every cry finds its own song,
In silence, we learn we belong.

So hold the noise within your chest,
And let it flow, but find your rest,
For in this dance of soft decay,
Silence whispers, come what may.

The Solace of Hidden Corners

In quiet spaces where shadows play,
Whispers of secrets in soft decay.
Time lingers softly, the world outside,
Finding the peace where thoughts can hide.

A delicate bloom in a forgotten nook,
Pages of stories in every look.
Nature's embrace in a silent plea,
Cradled in solace, just you and me.

Dust motes dance in the golden light,
Echoes of laughter that feel just right.
Soft as a sigh on a breezy morn,
In hidden corners, our dreams reborn.

Moss-covered stones in the gentle dusk,
Breath of the earth, a tender musk.
Here in stillness, we weave our thread,
Finding our peace where few have tread.

Let shadows cradle the worries we share,
In these hidden corners, free of care.
A tapestry woven of whispers and sighs,
Where love knows no limits and never dies.

Floating Through the Mysterious

Beneath the veil of the star-speckled sky,
A journey begins with a gentle sigh.
Waves of the cosmos pull us along,
In the dance of silence, we come to belong.

Gliding through twilight, we drift and weave,
Holding the echoes of dreams in reprieve.
What lies beyond is a question best asked,
As we float through the shadows, a wondrous task.

Moonlit pathways twinkle with grace,
In this realm of wonder, we find our place.
A delicate whisper calls us near,
Orbs of the unknown, shimmering clear.

Softly we sail on a current unseen,
Painting the night with a hue of serene.
Every heartbeat a compass, we flow,
In the mystery's arms, together we grow.

The universe beckons with secrets untold,
Stories of stardust in realms to behold.
Floating through echoes of ages gone by,
In the quilt of existence, we learn to fly.

Harmonies of the Unheard

In notes of silence, the world does sing,
Echoes of beauty in every spring.
The flutter of wings in the quiet air,
Melodies linger, tender and rare.

Beneath the surface, where shadows reside,
Lies a symphony, concealed and wide.
The rustle of leaves holds a secret chord,
Calling us close to the unheard reward.

Soft whispers of dawn in delicate hues,
Paint the horizon with subtle muse.
Every heartbeat, a rhythm of time,
Binding our spirits in gentle rhyme.

Listen closely to the world's soft sigh,
Mirrors of wonder reflect in the sky.
In harmonies hidden, we find our way,
Trusting the echoes that guide our stay.

Together we dance in the spaces between,
Crafting a ballet of moments unseen.
With every step, we harmoniously tread,
In the silence where music is born and bred.

Sighs of a Sleeping World

In the hush of twilight, the day says goodbye,
Cradled in night's arms, the stars start to sigh.
Dreams linger softly on the edge of sleep,
While secrets of evening in silence we keep.

Mountains stand guard as the shadows reform,
Embracing the stillness, the calm before storms.
A whispering breeze carries tales of the night,
Where hearts take flight in the soft, fading light.

Glimmers of moonlight on valleys so deep,
Woven in slumber, the world starts to weep.
Each droplet of dew, a kiss from above,
Scent of the earth, where we learn how to love.

The hush of the night guards our cherished dreams,
Wrapped in the fabric of soft moonbeams.
In the sighs of a world that is quiet and wise,
We drift into stillness, with stars in our eyes.

Let the night cradle the whispers of bliss,
In the arms of the dark lies a tender kiss.
Tomorrow will come with its own light and swirl,
But for now, we rest in a sleeping world.

Milton Keynes UK
Ingram Content Group UK Ltd.
UKHW020038271124
451585UK00012B/911

"In the Quiet" invites readers on an introspective journey through the serene landscapes of silence and stillness. Each poem encapsulates moments of solitude, where the soft whispers of nature intermingle with the stirring depths of human emotion.

With delicate imagery and profound reflections, the collection explores themes of love, loss, hope, and renewal. The verses encourage readers to embrace the beauty found in the pauses of life, celebrating the power of quiet moments to reveal inner truths and spark creativity.

Whether wandering through a tranquil forest or contemplating the stars on a calm night, "In the Quiet" is a soothing companion that beckons us to listen closely, unveiling the melodies that resonate in the silence.

ISBN 978-9916-89-983-0